Wonders

McGraw Hill

Cover and Title Page: Nathan Love

www.mheonline.com/readingwonders

Mc Graw Hill

Send all inquiries to:
McGraw-Hill Education
2 Penn Plaza
New York, NY 10121

ISBN: 978-0-02-130159-1
MHID: 0-02-130159-X

Printed in the United States of America

10 11 LKV 27 26 25   E

Wonders

ELD
Companion Worktext

Program Authors

Diane August

Jana Echevarria

Josefina V. Tinajero

McGraw Hill

THAT'S THE Spirit!

The Big Idea

THAT'S THE Spirit!

THE Big Idea

How can you show your community spirit?

3

Weekly Concept Friendship

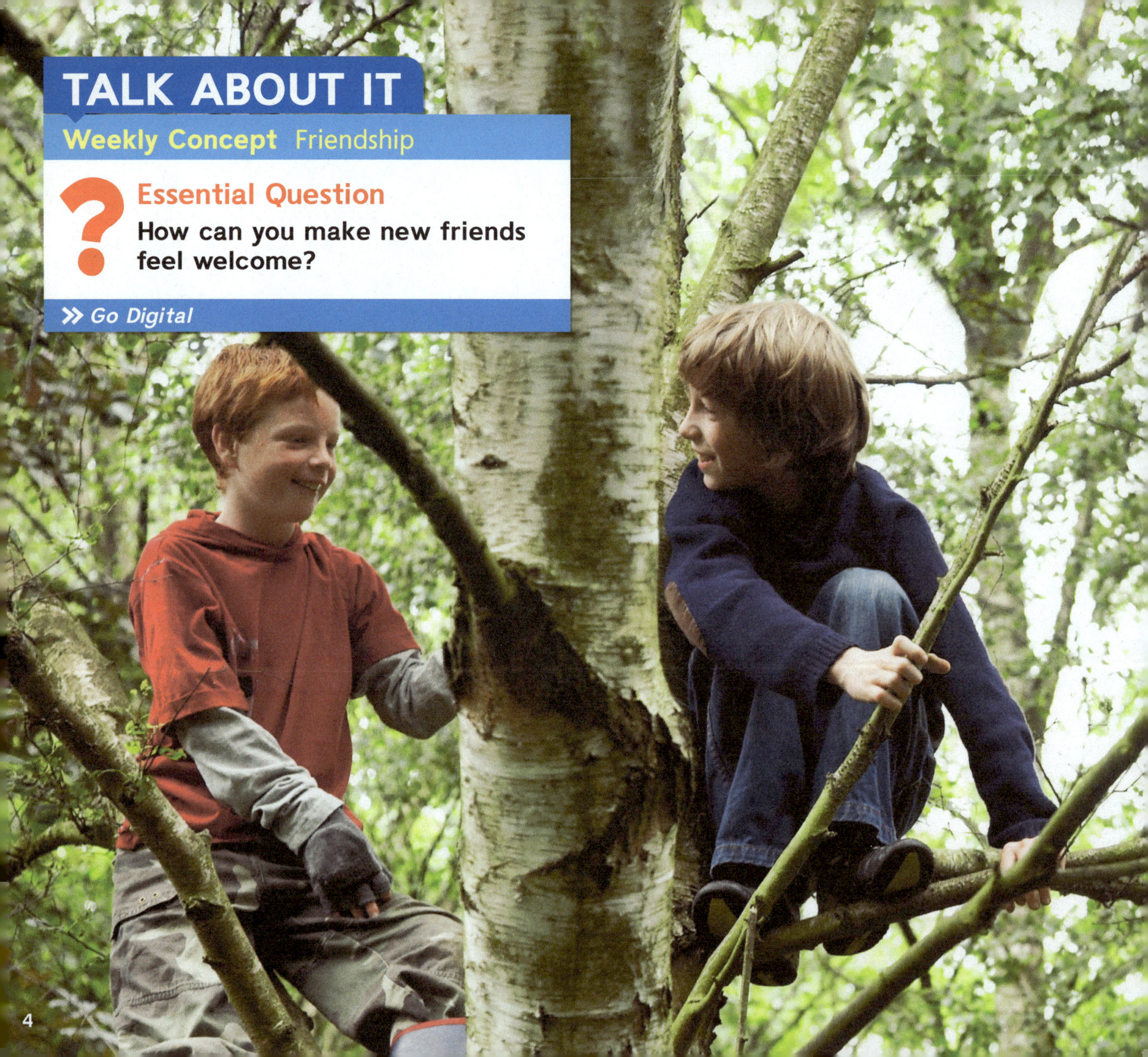

? **Essential Question**
How can you make new friends feel welcome?

>> *Go Digital*

What are the boys doing? Describe what friends do together. Write the words in the chart.

```
┌──────────────┐   ┌──────────────┐   ┌──────────────┐
│              │   │              │   │              │
│              │   │              │   │              │
│              │   │              │   │              │
└──────┬───────┘   └──────┬───────┘   └──────┬───────┘
       │                  │                  │
        ↘                 ↓                 ↙
        ┌─────────────────────────────────────┐
        │                                     │
        │                                     │
        │           Making Friends            │
        │                                     │
        │                                     │
        └─────────────────────────────────────┘
```

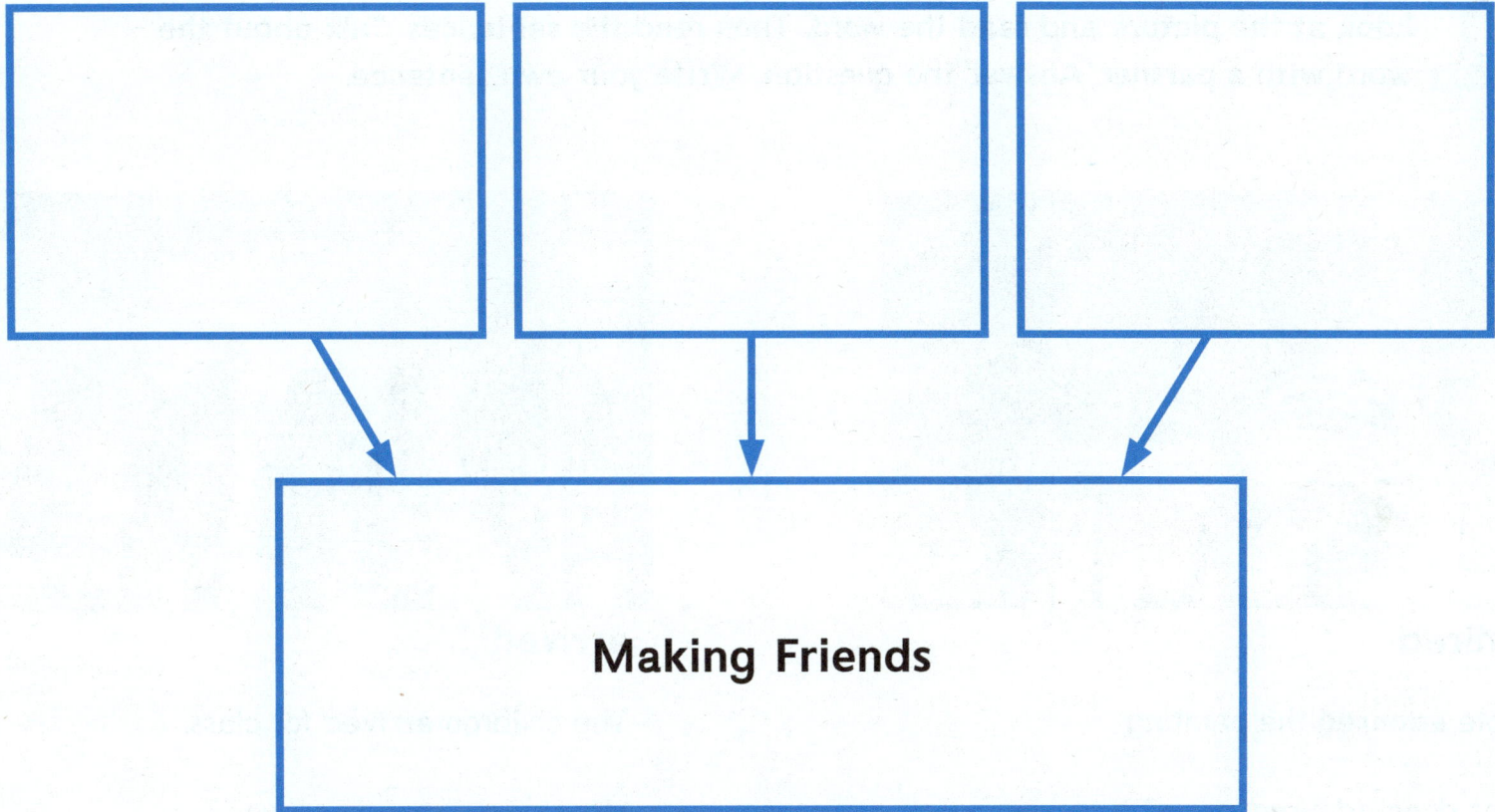

Discuss how each boy can welcome a new friend. Use the words from the chart. You can say:

The boy can make a new friend feel welcome by _____.

More Vocabulary

Look at the picture and read the word. Then read the sentences. Talk about the word with a partner. Answer the question. Write your own sentence.

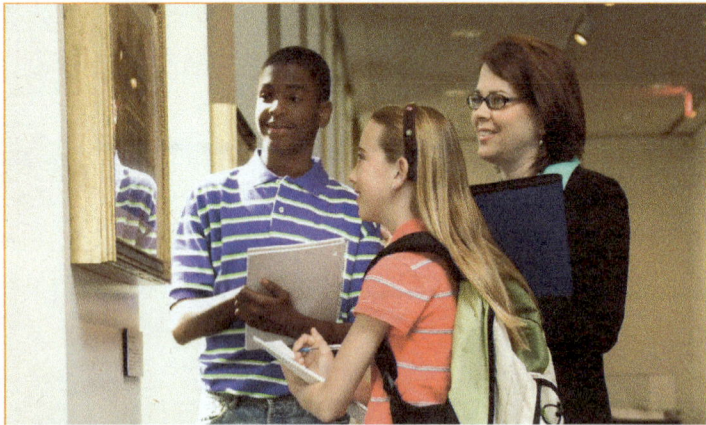

admired

People **admired** the painting.

What does *admired* mean?

| liked | laughed | hated |

Why is the painting admired?

The painting is admired because _____.

arrived

The children **arrived** for class.

What word means *arrived?*

| left | came | stopped |

When did you arrive at school?

I arrived at school at _____.

6

Words and Phrases: Phrasal Verbs

bent down = moved the body lower

The girl **bent down** to pet the dog.

face down = the front of someone or something that is facing downward and not showing

The swimmer holds her breath when she is **face down** in the water.

COLLABORATE Talk with a partner. Look at the pictures. Read the sentences. Write the word that completes the sentence.

The boy _____ to tie his shoe.
face down   bent down

The tiles are _____ on the table.
bent down   face down

COLLABORATE

1 Talk About It

Look at the picture. Read the title. Discuss what you see. Use these words.

book   library   man   small

Write about what you see.

I see _____

_____ .

Who are the people you see?

The people are _____

_____ .

What is the man doing?

The man is _____

_____ .

Take notes as you read the text.

At the Library

Essential Question

?   **How can you make new friends feel welcome?**

Read how a new librarian and an unlikely family become great friends.

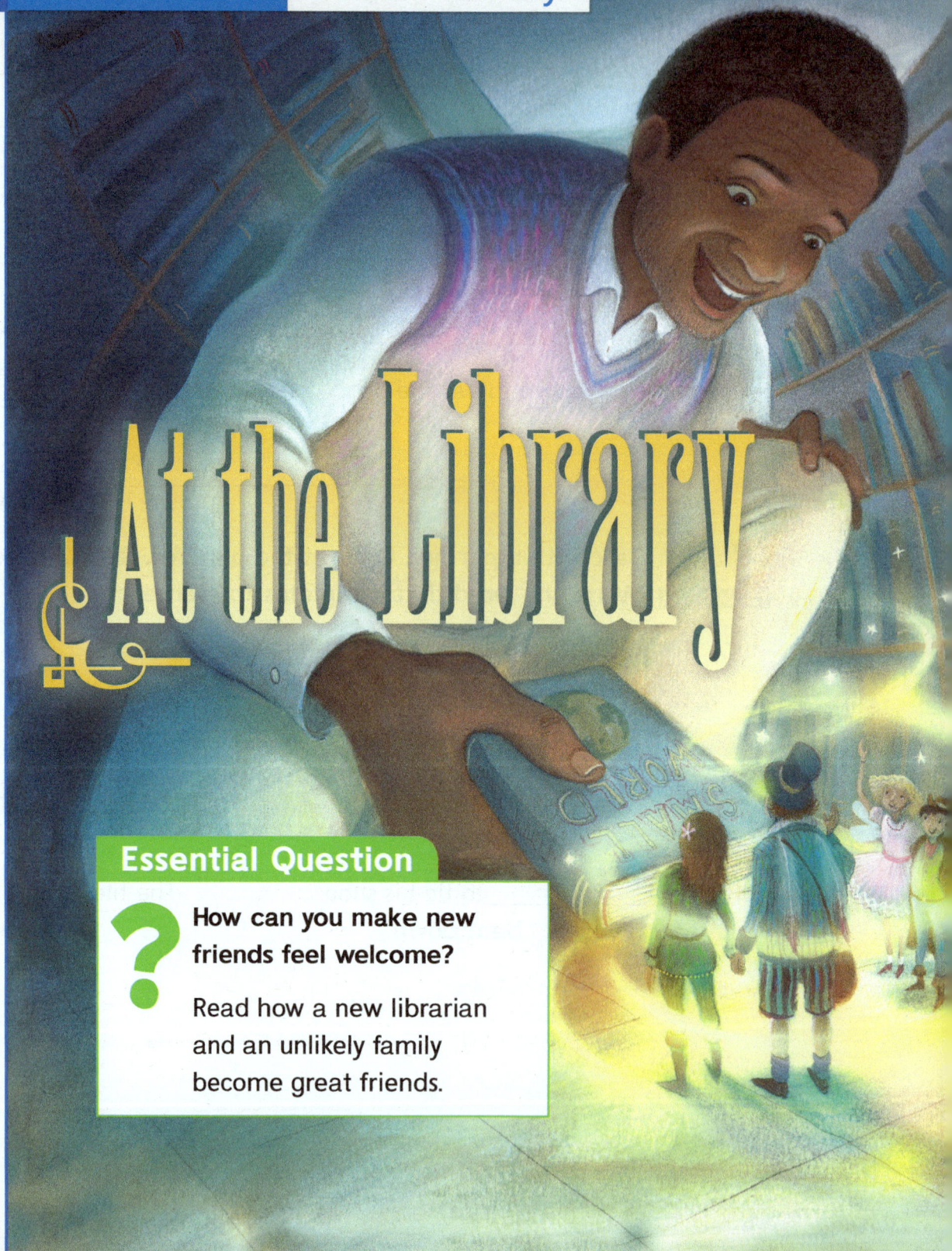

Rick Dodson worked in a library. It was the end of the work day, as Rick **admired** the beautiful orange sun setting behind the Blue Ridge Mountains. He was about to leave but saw a pile of books on a table. Rick began putting the books away but suddenly stopped.

"No, not tonight," Rick said. Librarians always put away books, but today was Rick's birthday. So instead Rick went to the Cupcake Café for a birthday treat.

Afterward, Rick went home. Sitting in his living room, Rick was thinking about his old friends. They had just phoned to wish him a happy birthday. If only this job wasn't so far away from his friends. The library job **required** Rick to move across the country. Now, after six months, he had made a few new acquaintances but no real friends.

"Books are my friends," thought Rick. Then he remembered the books he left on the table at the library. Rick decided to return to the library and put the books away.

As Rick entered the library, he noticed a book, *Small World,* face down on the floor. "This wasn't here before. What's going on?" Rick said. Then he bent down and picked up the book.

Just then Rick saw four tiny figures on the floor. "Ahhh," he yelled and dropped the book.

The tiny people hurried out of the way as the book fell to the floor. A little man said, "Mr. Dodson, we're pleased to meet you."

"Who are you?" Rick asked with great surprise.

Richard Johnson

❶ Comprehension

Point of View

Someone is telling this story. That person is called a third-person narrator. The story has the words *he, him, his, she, her,* and *hers.* Reread the third paragraph. Underline the sentences that tell you that the narrator thinks Rick is lonely.

❷ Specific Vocabulary Ⓐ Ⓒ Ⓣ

In the third paragraph, find the word *required.* The word *required* means "needed to do something." What was Rick required to do for his job?

Rick was required to _____

_____.

❸ Sentence Structure Ⓐ Ⓒ Ⓣ

Reread the first sentence in the fifth paragraph. Circle the punctuation marks. Underline the title of the book on the floor.

Text Evidence 🔍

1 Sentence Structure Ⓐ Ⓒ Ⓣ

Reread the first paragraph. Circle the sentence that tells you who is speaking. Underline the names of the Booker children.

2 Specific Vocabulary Ⓐ Ⓒ Ⓣ

Reread the third paragraph. The word *file* means "a set of papers that gives information about a person or thing." Underline the words that give you a clue to the meaning of *file*.

COLLABORATE

3 Talk About It

Discuss how the Bookers make sure everything runs smoothly in the library. Then write about it.

The Bookers make sure things run

smoothly by _____

_____

_____.

"We're the Bookers! I am William. This is Emily and our children, Harry and Clementine. By the way, happy birthday!"

"You know it's my birthday?" Rick asked.

"We read your **file** when you **arrived** because we wanted to learn about the new librarian," said William.

Rick collapsed into a nearby chair and rubbed his eyes. He could not believe what he was seeing.

Then, the Bookers climbed up the table. "You can trust us," said Emily.

"Every library has Bookers!" William said.

"We make sure everything runs smoothly. We keep the mice away. They chew on everything," Emily said.

"I do a mouse patrol every night," said Harry proudly.

Clementine said, "We oil the chairs and sharpen the pencils, too."

Rick asked the Bookers, "But why do you do this work?"

"We work and read. Bookers and libraries belong together!" said William.

"Mr. Dodson, we want to be your friends," said Emily.

Rick Dodson **grinned**, "Call me, Rick. And I'd love to be your friend."

Rick made other friends, but he spent many evenings with the Bookers, too. Every year on his birthday, Rick brought cupcakes to share with the Bookers.

Make Connections

? Talk about how the Bookers made Rick Dodson feel welcome.
ESSENTIAL QUESTION

How do you make new students in your school feel welcome?
TEXT TO SELF

Text Evidence

1 Sentence Structure A C T

Reread the first sentence in the first paragraph. Circle the pronoun. Then find the word in the second sentence that can replace the pronoun *we*. Rewrite the sentence using the word.

_____ work and read.

2 Specific Vocabulary A C T

Reread the third paragraph. The word *grinned* means "smiled." Why did Rick grin?

Rick grinned because _____.

COLLABORATE

3 Talk About It

Discuss how Rick's life changes from the beginning of the story and by the end of the story.

In the beginning, Rick was _____

_____.

By the end, Rick was _____

_____.

11

Respond to the Text

Partner Discussion Work with a partner. Read the questions about "At the Library." Show where you found the text evidence. Write the page numbers. Then describe what you learned.

What did you learn about Rick at the beginning of the story?

I read that Rick moved _____.

In the story, Rick has not made _____.

I read that Rick loves _____.

Text Evidence

Page(s): _____

Page(s): _____

Page(s): _____

What did you learn about the Bookers?

I read that the Bookers are _____.

In the text, the Bookers take care of _____.

I read the Bookers also love _____.

Text Evidence

Page(s): _____

Page(s): _____

Page(s): _____

Group Discussion Present your answers to the class. Cite text evidence for your ideas. Listen to and discuss the group's opinions about your ideas.

I think your idea is _____.

Write Work with a partner. Look at your notes about "At the Library." Then write your answer to the essential question. Use text evidence to support your answer. Use vocabulary words in your writing.

How did the Bookers make Rick feel welcome?

The Bookers looked at Rick's file because _____

_____.

The Bookers take care of the library by _____

_____.

At the end of the story, the Bookers ask Rick to _____

_____.

Share Writing Present your writing to the class. Then talk about their opinions. Talk about their ideas. Explain why you agree or disagree with their ideas. You can say:

I agree with _____.

I do not agree because _____.

Write to Sources

Take Notes About the Text I took notes on the idea web about the story. It will help me respond to the prompt: *Have William write a letter to another family of Bookers. Tell them about Rick Dodson. Use details from the story.*

Shaun

pages 8–11

Detail
At first, we surprised him.

Detail
He wanted to be friends.

Main Idea
Rick Dodson is the new librarian.

Detail
He spends many evenings with us.

Detail
He shares birthday cupcakes with us.

Write About the Text I used my notes from my idea web to write a letter. The letter is to other Bookers from William. The letter tells about Rick Dodson.

Student Model: *Narrative Text*

Dear Lake Vista Library Bookers,

We met our new librarian. His name is Rick Dodson. At first, we surprised him. Then he said he wanted to be friends. He spends many evenings at the library. He spends them with us. Best of all, he shares cupcakes with us on his birthday. We like our librarian.

Your friend,

William

TALK ABOUT IT

COLLABORATE

Text Evidence
Draw a box around a sentence from the notes that tells how Rick felt when he met the Bookers. Does it tell what happened first?

Grammar
Circle an action verb. Why did Shaun use action verbs?

Condense Ideas
Underline the two sentences that tell how Rick spends his evenings. How can you condense the two sentences into one detailed sentence?

Your Turn
COLLABORATE

Pretend you are Rick Dodson. Write a letter about the Bookers to a friend. Use details from the story.

>> *Go Digital*
Write your response online. Use your editing checklist.

? **Essential Question**
In what ways can you help your community?

>> *Go Digital*

What are the girls doing? How are they helping their community? Write words in the idea web.

Helping the Community

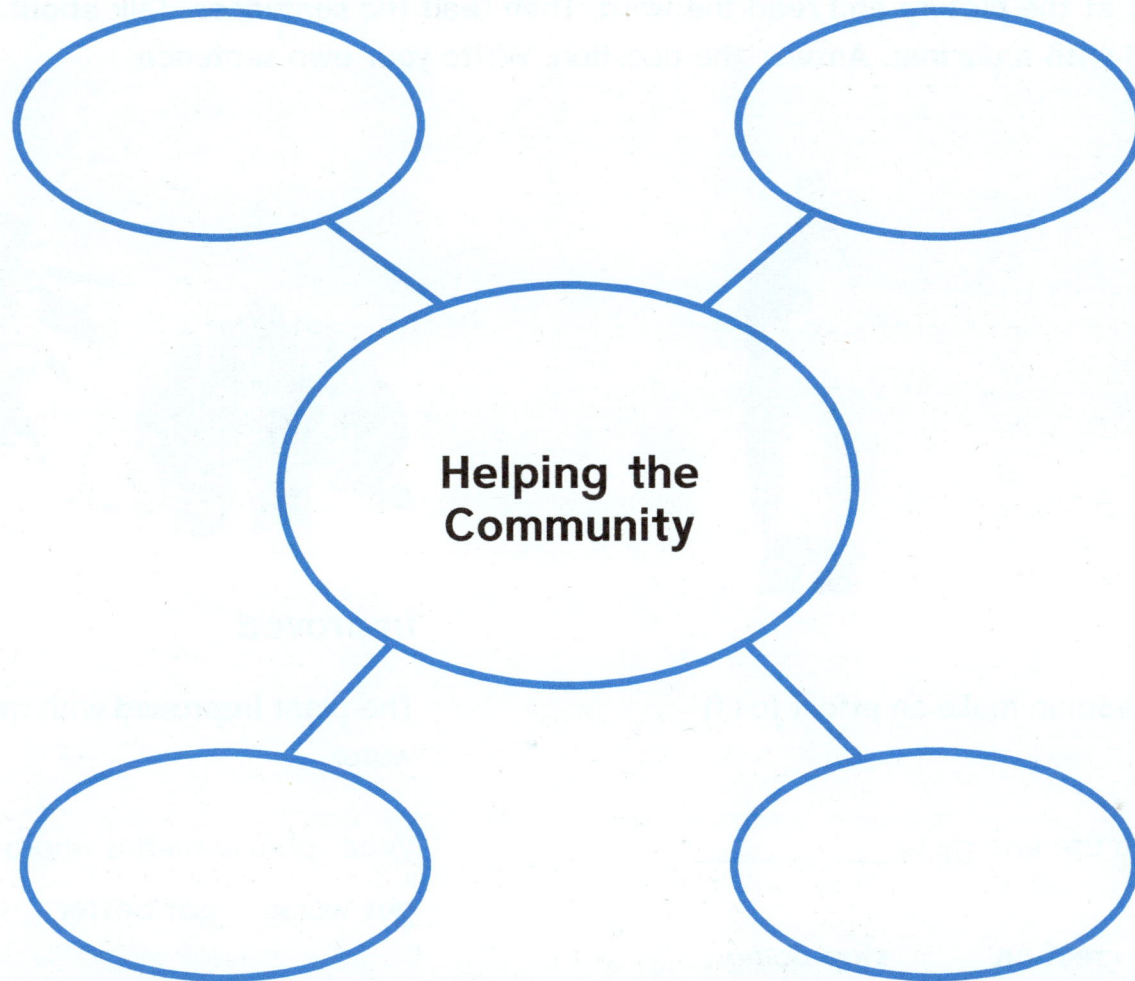

Look at the photo of the girls. Discuss how you can help your community. Use the words from the idea web. You can say:

I can help to _____. I can also help to _____.

More Vocabulary

Look at the picture and read the word. Then read the sentences. Talk about the word with a partner. Answer the question. Write your own sentence.

COLLABORATE

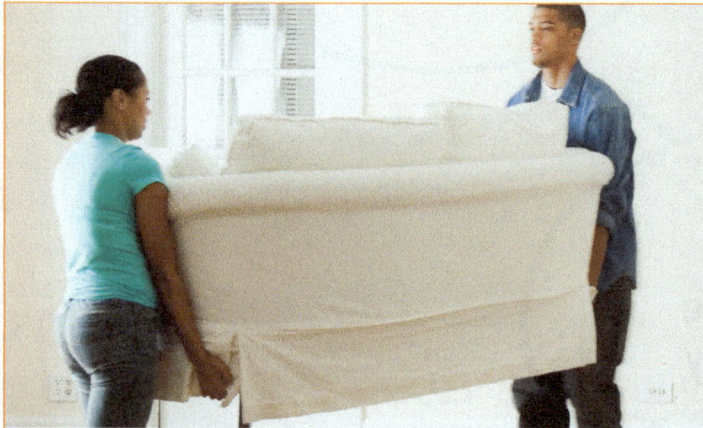

effort

The man and woman make an **effort** to lift the couch.

Effort means to use energy to _____ something.

try to do   rest on   stop doing

What do you make an effort to do?

I make an effort to _____.

improved

The plant **improved** with more sun and water.

What phrase means *improved?*

got worse   got better   stayed the same

What did you improve this year?

I improved my _____.

Words and Phrases: Prepositions *over* and *across*

A preposition is a word that tells where something is located.

Where is the teacher leaning?

The teacher is leaning **over** the desk.

Where does the bridge go?

The bridge goes **across** the water.

 Talk with a partner. Look at the pictures. Read the sentences. Write the word that completes the sentence.

COLLABORATE

The blanket goes _____ the boy's head.

over   across

The people walked _____ the street.

over   across

COLLABORATE

1 Talk About It

Look at the photograph. Read the title. Discuss what you see. Use these words.

storm   people   driving

Write about what you see.

I see _____

_____.

Where is the person telling the story?

The person telling the story is _____

_____.

What are the people outside doing?

The people outside are _____

_____.

Take notes as you read the story.

REMEMBERING HURRICANE KATRINA

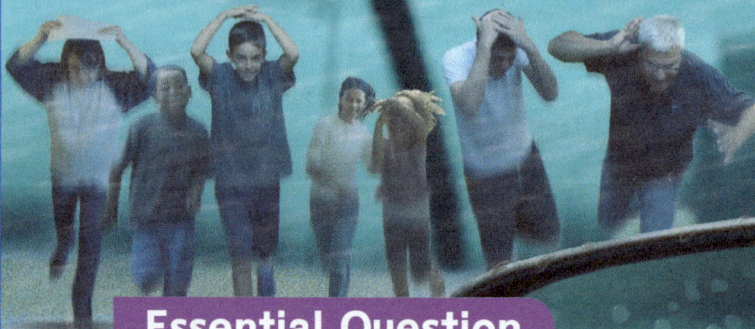

Essential Question

? **In what ways can you help your community?**

Read about how Hector helps others after Hurricane Katrina.

As I was driving, the sky was getting darker. I leaned over my steering wheel and saw heavy rain clouds. A storm was coming. I **glanced** at the boxes of clothes in the back seat. I was donating them to people in need.

Raindrops were scattered across my windshield. I pulled the car off the road until the weather **improved**. People outside held their hands over their heads in an **effort** to keep from getting too wet. The heavy rain reminded me of another big storm years earlier.

Hurricane Katrina hit the Gulf Coast of the United States when I was nine years old. The powerful storm caused a lot of damage.

I remember watching the news with Aunt Lucia. A reporter stood inside the Houston Astrodome, in Texas, where there were thousands of people. The people were tired and sad. Many people wore torn and dirty clothes, and some had no shoes on their feet.

Text Evidence

❶ Specific Vocabulary Ⓐ Ⓒ Ⓣ

Reread the fourth sentence in the first paragraph. The word *glanced* means "looked at quickly." Circle the words that tell what Hector glanced at. Rewrite the sentence using a different word for glanced.

I _____ at the boxes of

clothes in the back seat.

❷ Comprehension

Reread the last paragraph. What does Hector remember about Hurricane Katrina?

Hector remembers _____

_____

_____.

❸ Sentence Structure Ⓐ Ⓒ Ⓣ

Reread the last sentence in the last paragraph. Circle the word that connects the two parts of the sentence. Underline the two parts. These parts are complete sentences.

Text Evidence

1 Sentence Structure A C T

Reread the second sentence in the second paragraph. Circle the pronoun *they*. Underline the word in the first paragraph that the pronoun *they* refers to.

2 Comprehension
Point of View

Reread the fourth paragraph. Underline the details that tell why Hector felt he had to do something to help the people in the Astrodome.

3 Specific Vocabulary A C T

Reread the second sentence in the last paragraph. The word *devised* means "came up with a way to do something." Circle the words that tell you what Hector and his friends devised. Underline the sentence that tells why they devised the plan.

I asked Aunt Lucia, "Are the people in Houston because of the hurricane?"

Aunt Lucia explained, "*Sí*, Hector. They are from New Orleans, Louisiana. Hurricane Katrina destroyed their homes. They lost everything. For now, they are temporary residents of the Astrodome until it is safe to go home."

Hurricane Katrina came very close to Texas. I was worried the storm would strike us in Houston but it missed us. Other cities were not so lucky.

The news reporter was interviewing people. I noticed a little boy sitting behind her. He was hugging an old teddy bear. I knew I had to do something.

The next day, I met with my friends at the volunteer club, the Houston Helpers. We **devised** a plan to collect toys for the kids at the Astrodome. We wanted to donate toys to give the children a little joy.

We told everyone in our schools and in other organizations. Three days later, the donation boxes were filled with new toys!

I'll never forget the day we went to the Astrodome with our gifts. Children smiled as we pulled toys from our bags. Their parents thanked us for our generosity.

Then my cell phone rang and brought me back to the present. I noticed that the storm had passed.

"Hector?"

"Hi, Jeannie," I answered.

"Do you have the clothing donations? The tornado yesterday destroyed many homes. Many people need help," Jeannie said.

I answered, "Yes, I have the clothing donations. The storm delayed me, but I'll be there soon!"

I drove my car into the busy traffic. It felt good to know that I was making a difference again.

Make Connections

? Talk about how Hector and his friends make a difference in their community. **ESSENTIAL QUESTION**

What are some things that you have done to help your school or community? **TEXT TO SELF**

Text Evidence

1 Sentence Structure **ACT**

Reread the first sentence in the third paragraph. Circle the word that connects the two actions in the sentence. Underline the words that tell what happened after Hector's cell phone rang.

COLLABORATE

2 Talk About It

Talk about whom Hector is helping with the clothing donations. Then write about it.

The clothing donations will help

_____

_____

3 Comprehension
Point of View

Reread the last paragraph. How did Hector feel about helping people in need?

Hector felt _____

_____.

Respond to the Text

Partner Discussion Work with a partner. Read the questions about "Remembering Hurricane Katrina." Show where you found the text evidence. Write the page numbers. Then describe what you learned.

What did Hector do to help people after Hurricane Katrina?

Hector and his friends had a club called _____.   Page(s): _____

They devised a plan to _____.   Page(s): _____

They wanted to give the children _____.   Page(s): _____

Text Evidence

What did Hector do to help people after a tornado?

Hector was driving to _____.   Page(s): _____

In his car, he had _____.   Page(s): _____

Hector feels good about _____.   Page(s): _____

Text Evidence

Group Discussion Present your answers to the class. Cite text evidence for your ideas. Listen to and discuss the group's opinions about your ideas.

I think your idea is _____.

Write Work with a partner. Look at your notes about "Remembering Hurricane Katrina." Then write your answer to the essential question. Use text evidence to support your answer. Use vocabulary words in your writing.

How do Hector and his friends help their community?

After Hurricane Katrina, Hector and his friends helped children by _____

_____.

After a recent tornado, Hector and his friends helped by _____

_____.

Hector feels good about helping others because he says _____

_____.

Share Writing Present your writing to the class. Then talk about their opinions. Think about their ideas. Explain why you agree or disagree with their ideas. You can say:

I agree with _____.

I do not agree because _____.

Ava

Take Notes About the Text I took notes on the chart about what I know about the selection. It will help me to respond to the prompt: *Pretend you are Hector. Tell what it was like to give out toys at the Astrodome.*

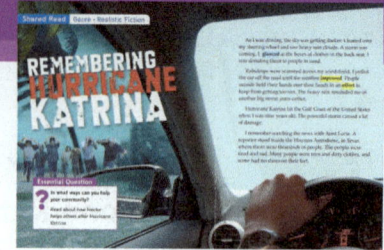

REMEMBERING HURRICANE KATRINA

pages 20–23

Hector saw on TV many people at the Houston Astrodome because of Hurricane Katrina.

The hurricane destroyed their homes. People were tired and sad.

Hector and his friends devised a plan to collect toys for the kids.

Children smiled and their parents thanked Hector and his friends for the toys.

Write About the Text I used my notes to write a paragraph about what it was like for Hector to give out toys at the Astrodome.

Student Model: *Narrative Text*

There were many people at the Astrodome when we arrived. They were there because of Hurricane Katrina. They had lost everything. We had bags of toys we collected. The kids flew toward us. When we pulled toys from our bags, the kids smiled. The parents were glad we were there. They thanked us. I felt happy to help.

COLLABORATE

TALK ABOUT IT

Text Evidence

Draw a box around a detail from the notes that tells why there were so many people at the Astrodome. Does the sentence tell about the cause or the effect?

Grammar

Circle a past-tense verb. Why did Ava use the past tense?

Connect Ideas

Underline the second and third sentences. How can the sentences be connected using the word *and?*

COLLABORATE

Your Turn

Pretend you are a kid at the Astrodome. Tell about how you felt when you received toys. Use details from the selection.

>> Go Digital
Write your response online. Use your editing checklist.

Weekly Concept Liberty and Justice

? **Essential Question**

How can one person make a difference?

>> *Go Digital*

How do superheroes in stories help people? How can you help people in your community? Write words in the chart.

Make a Difference

Discuss how you can make a difference. Use the words from the chart. You can say:

I can _____. I can also _____ others.

More Vocabulary

Look at the picture and read the word. Then read the sentences. Talk about the word with a partner. Answer the question. Write your own sentence.

afford

They can **afford** to buy a plant.

The word *afford* means _____ to do something.

not able   not going   is able

What can you afford to do?

I can afford to _____

_____.

destroyed

The building is being **destroyed**.

What is the meaning of *destroyed*?

broken down   fixed up   protected by

Why do you think the building is being destroyed?

The building is being destroyed because

_____

_____.

Words and Phrases: Phrasal Verbs

held up = raised something up in the air.

They **held up** the award to show everyone.

grew up = the place where a person spent time as a child

The girl **grew up** in a big city.

COLLABORATE Talk with a partner. Look at the pictures. Read the sentences. Write the phrasal verb that completes each sentence.

The boy _____ his hand.

grew up   **held up**

My friend _____ on a farm.

grew up   **held up**

COLLABORATE

1 Talk About It

Look at the photograph. Read the title. Discuss what you see. Use these words.

mountaintop   woman   change

Write about what you see.

I see _____

_____.

What does the mountaintop look like?

The mountaintop looks like _____

_____.

What is the woman doing?

She is _____

_____.

Take notes as you read the text.

Judy's APPALACHIA

Essential Question

? **How can one person make a difference?**

Read about how one person decided to take a stand.

A mountaintop is removed to mine for coal in Appalachia.

Judy Bonds and her grandson stood in a creek in West Virginia. He held up a handful of dead fish. "What's wrong with these fish?" he asked. That day changed Judy's life forever. She decided to fight against the coal mining companies that were harming her home.

Marfork, West Virginia

Judy Bonds was the daughter of a coal miner. The people of Marfork had been coal miners for many years. Coal gave people the energy they needed to light and warm their homes.

Marfork was also home to a leafy green valley. The valley was surrounded by the Appalachian Mountains on every side. Judy's family had lived in Marfork for a long time.

Mountaintop Removal Mining

An energy company came to Marfork in the 1990s. It began a process called mountaintop removal mining. Using dynamite, the company blew off the tops of mountains to get to the coal under them. The process was fast, but it caused many problems. Whole forests were destroyed.

Judy Bonds spoke out against mountaintop removal mining.

Text Evidence

1 Sentence Structure A C T

Reread the first sentence in the first paragraph. Circle the subjects in the sentence. Underline the words that tell what the subjects are doing.

2 Comprehension

Reread the first paragraph. Underline a reason why Judy Bonds decided to fight against the coal mining companies.

3 Specific Vocabulary A C T

Reread the second sentence in the last paragraph. The word *process* means "actions that help to get something done." Underline the process the energy company used. Circle the problem that the process caused.

Text Evidence

1 Specific Vocabulary ⒶⒸⓉ

Reread the first sentence in the first paragraph. The word *explosions* means "loud sounds caused by something being blown apart." Underline the word that tells what caused the explosions. Circle the problem the explosions caused.

2 Sentence Structure ⒶⒸⓉ

Reread the third sentence in the first paragraph. Circle the commas. Underline the words that tell you what coal sludge is.

COLLABORATE

3 Talk About It

Reread the timeline. Circle the date when Judy was forced to leave her home. What fact on the timeline tells you that Judy was successful in helping to protect the land?

Judy was successful in helping to protect the land because she

_____

_____

Dust from the dynamite **explosions** filled the air. Dust covered the nearby towns. Coal sludge, a mixture of mud, chemicals, and coal dust, went into the creeks and rivers.

Pollution from the mining made people sick. In the area where Judy lived, coal sludge flowed into the rivers and streams. People packed up and moved. Judy and her family had to leave, too. Judy was heartbroken. The land she loved was being mistreated.

Working for Change

Judy decided to protest against mountaintop removal mining. She wanted the mining to stop. Judy felt she was able to talk to groups about the injustice. After all, she grew up in a mining family. The mining had forced people to move. Mountains and forests were being destroyed.

1952	2001	2003	2011
Judy is born in West Virginia.	Judy's family is forced to leave Marfork Hollow.	Judy is awarded the $150,000 Goldman Environmental Prize.	Judy dies at age 59.

Judy worked as a volunteer for a group that fought against mountaintop removal mining. She became a group leader. Judy led many protests against mining companies.

But at the protests, some miners were angry at Judy. Many coal miners supported the mining process because they needed the jobs. They could not **afford** to leave their jobs. So Judy began pushing for changes to the mining process. Slowly, small changes were made to protect communities in the mining areas.

Remembering Judy

Sadly, Judy did not meet all of her goals. She died in January 2011. But her success provided encouragement to others. Judy's work will protect the area and help others remain in their homes.

The Monongahela National Forest in West Virginia.

Make Connections

? How did Judy Bonds make a difference? ESSENTIAL QUESTION

What cause do you feel strongly about? TEXT TO SELF

(bkgd) Aimin Tang/R+/Getty Images; (bc) Courtesy Goldman Environmental Prize

Text Evidence

1 Sentence Structure A C T

Reread the third and fourth sentences in the second paragraph. Circle the word that connects the two sentences.

Rewrite the two sentences into

one sentence. _____

_____

_____.

COLLABORATE

2 Talk About It

Discuss the difference Judy made through her work. Then write about it.

Judy helped to change _____

_____

3 Comprehension

Author's Point of View

Reread the last paragraph. The author admires Judy Bonds for the work she did. Underline the details that tells you the author thinks Judy was successful.

Respond to the Text

Partner Discussion Work with a partner. Read the questions about "Judy's Appalachia." Show where you found the text evidence. Write the page numbers. Then describe what you learned.

COLLABORATE

How did mountaintop removal mining change Marfork?

Text Evidence 🔍

Before mountaintop removal mining, Marfork was _____.

Page(s): _____

Mountaintop removal mining destroyed the _____.

Page(s): _____

Pollution from the mining made people _____.

Page(s): _____

What did Judy Bonds do about mountaintop removal mining?

Text Evidence 🔍

Judy led many protests against _____.

Page(s): _____

Judy began pushing for changes to the _____.

Page(s): _____

The author says Judy's work will _____.

Page(s): _____

COLLABORATE

Group Discussion Present your answers to the group. Cite text evidence for your ideas. Listen to and discuss the group's opinions about your ideas.

I think your idea is _____.

Write Work with a partner. Look at your notes about "Judy's Appalachia." Then write your answer to the essential question. Use text evidence to support your answer. Use vocabulary words in your writing.

COLLABORATE

How did Judy Bonds make a difference?

Judy protested against _____

_____.

She pushed for changes in _____

_____.

Judy's work will help _____

_____.

Share Writing Present your writing to the class. Then talk about their opinions. Talk about their ideas. Explain why you agree or disagree with their ideas. You can say:

COLLABORATE

I agree with _____.

I do not agree because _____.

Write to Sources

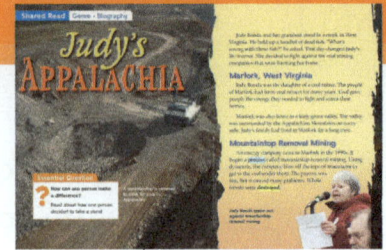

pages 32–35

Take Notes About the Text I took notes on the idea web to tell what I know about the selection. It will help me answer the question: *Was Judy's plan to change mining a good one?*

Sebastian

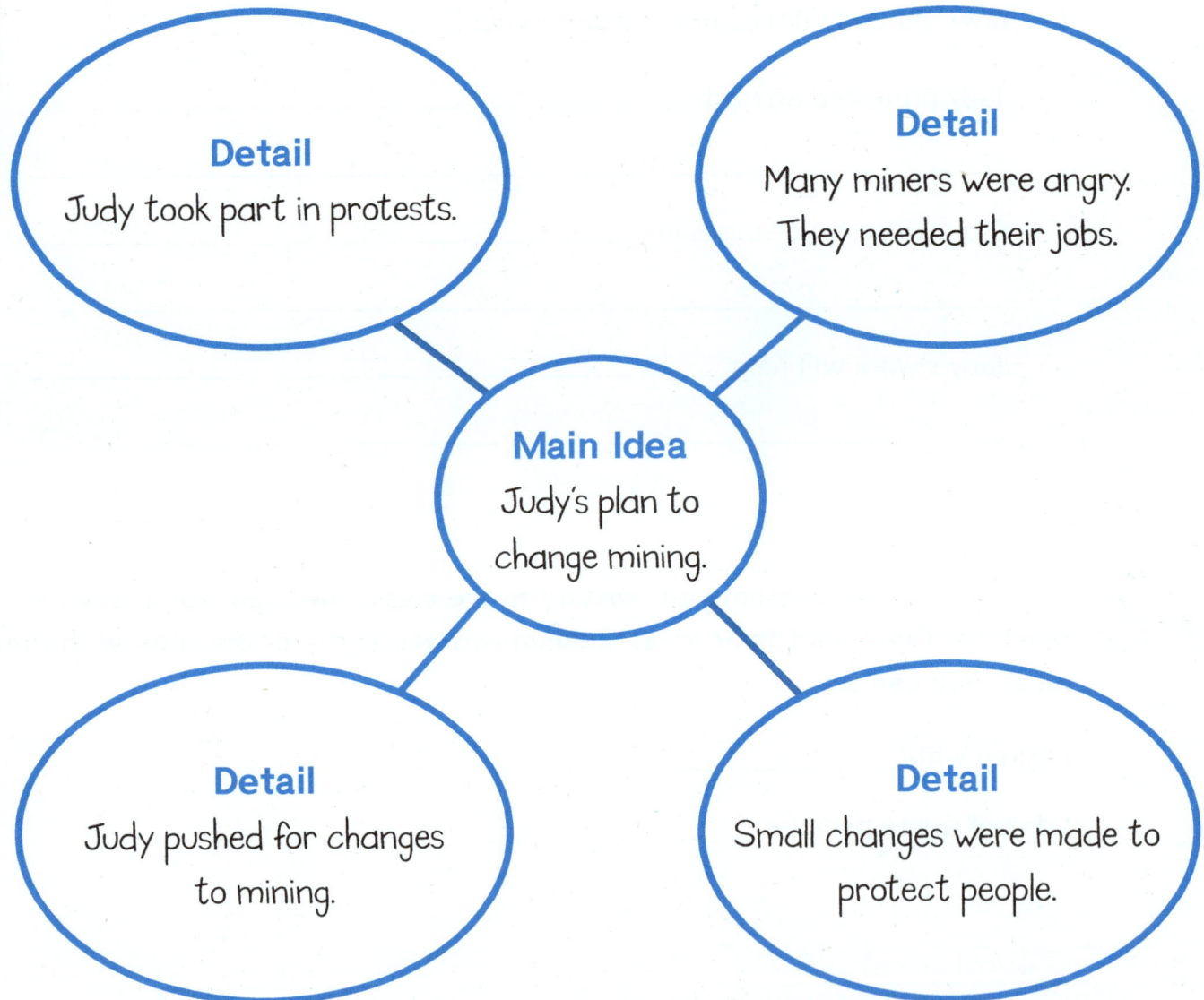

Detail
Judy took part in protests.

Detail
Many miners were angry. They needed their jobs.

Main Idea
Judy's plan to change mining.

Detail
Judy pushed for changes to mining.

Detail
Small changes were made to protect people.

Write About the Text I used notes from my idea web to write an opinion about Judy's plan to change mining.

Student Model: *Opinion*

Judy's plan to change mining was a good one. At first, Judy took part in protests. Many miners were angry. They needed their jobs. Instead she pushed for changes to mining. As a result, small changes were made to protect people. Judy's plan worked.

TALK ABOUT IT

Text Evidence

Draw a box around a supporting detail that comes from the notes. Does this detail support Sebastian's opinion?

Grammar

Circle a sentence that adds a detail to show when something happened. Is this detail at the beginning or the end of the sentence?

Connect Ideas

Underline the second and third sentences. How could you make the two sentences into one sentence using the word *but?*

Your Turn

Do you think the miners were right to be angry with Judy? Use text evidence.

>> Go Digital
Write your response online. Use your editing checklist.

39

? **Essential Question**

How can words lead to change?

>> *Go Digital*

"Education is the most powerful weapon which you can use to change the world."

–NELSON MANDELA

40

Describe what the man in the photograph is doing? How did his words lead to change? Write words in the chart.

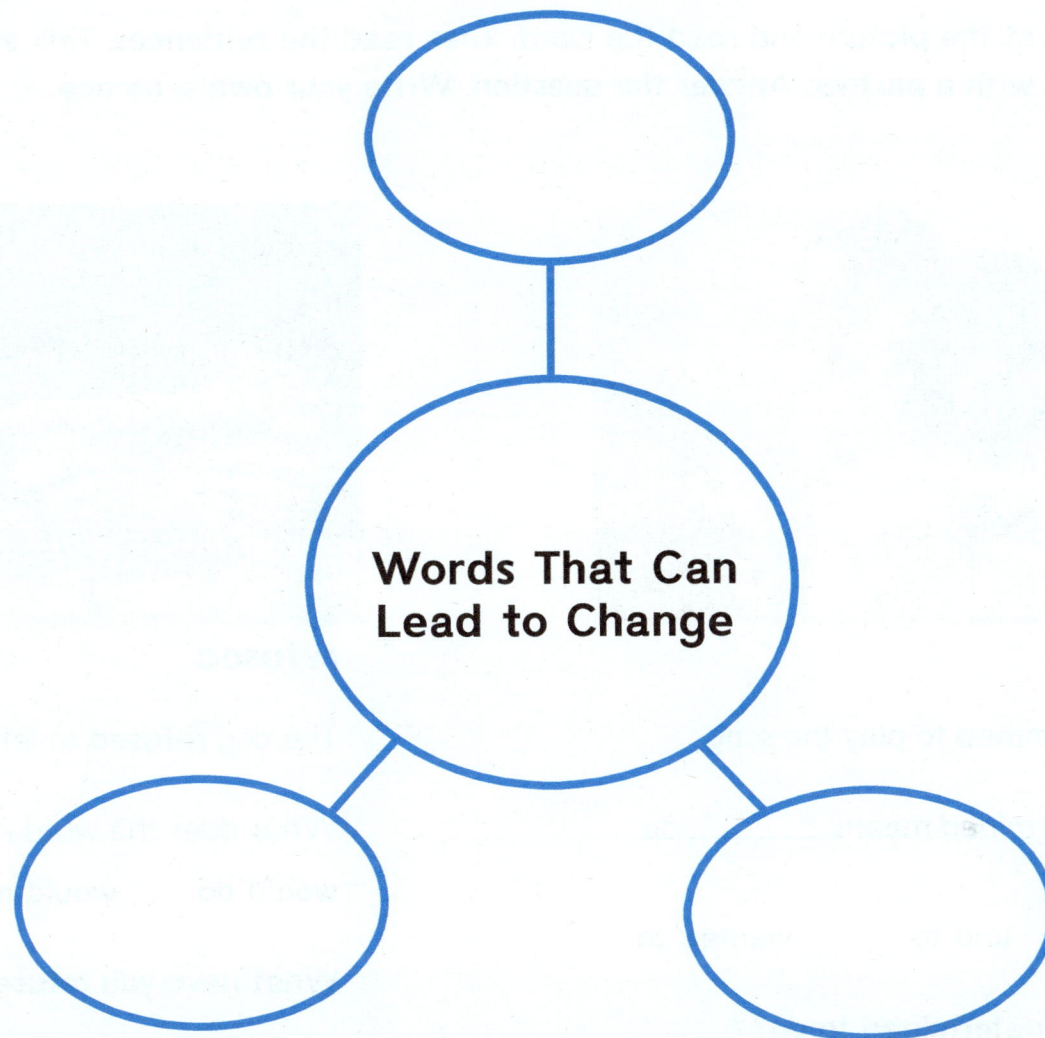

Words That Can Lead to Change

Discuss how words can lead to change. Use the words from the chart. You can say:

Words can _____ and _____.

More Vocabulary

(l)IT Stock Free/Alamy; (r)Compassionate Eye Foundation/Jetta Productions/Getty Images

COLLABORATE Look at the picture and read the word. Then read the sentences. Talk about the word with a partner. Answer the question. Write your own sentence.

determined

She was **determined** to play the song.

The word *determined* means _____ do something.

didn't want to   told to   wanted to

What are you determined to do?

I am determined to _____

_____.

refused

The dog **refused** to let go of the rope.

What does the word *refused* mean?

would do   would not do   did later

What have you refused to do?

I have refused to _____

_____.

Words and Phrases: Prefixes *in-* and *un-*

A prefix has letters added to the beginning of a word. It changes the meaning of a word.

The prefix *in-* means "not."

inactive = not active

Who is *inactive?*

The boy is **inactive** because he is napping.

The prefix *un-* means "not."

unhappy = not happy

Who is *unhappy?*

The boy is **unhappy** because he dropped the pail.

COLLABORATE Talk with a partner. Look at the pictures. Read the sentences. Write the word that completes the sentence.

The sheep are _____.

inactive   active

Ana's brother is _____.

happy   unhappy

COLLABORATE

① Talk About It

Look at the photograph. Read the title. Discuss what you see. Use these words.

women   march   signs

Write about what you see.

I see _____

_____ .

What are the women doing?

The women are _____

_____ .

What do the women want?

They want _____

_____ .

Take notes as you read the text.

Words for Change

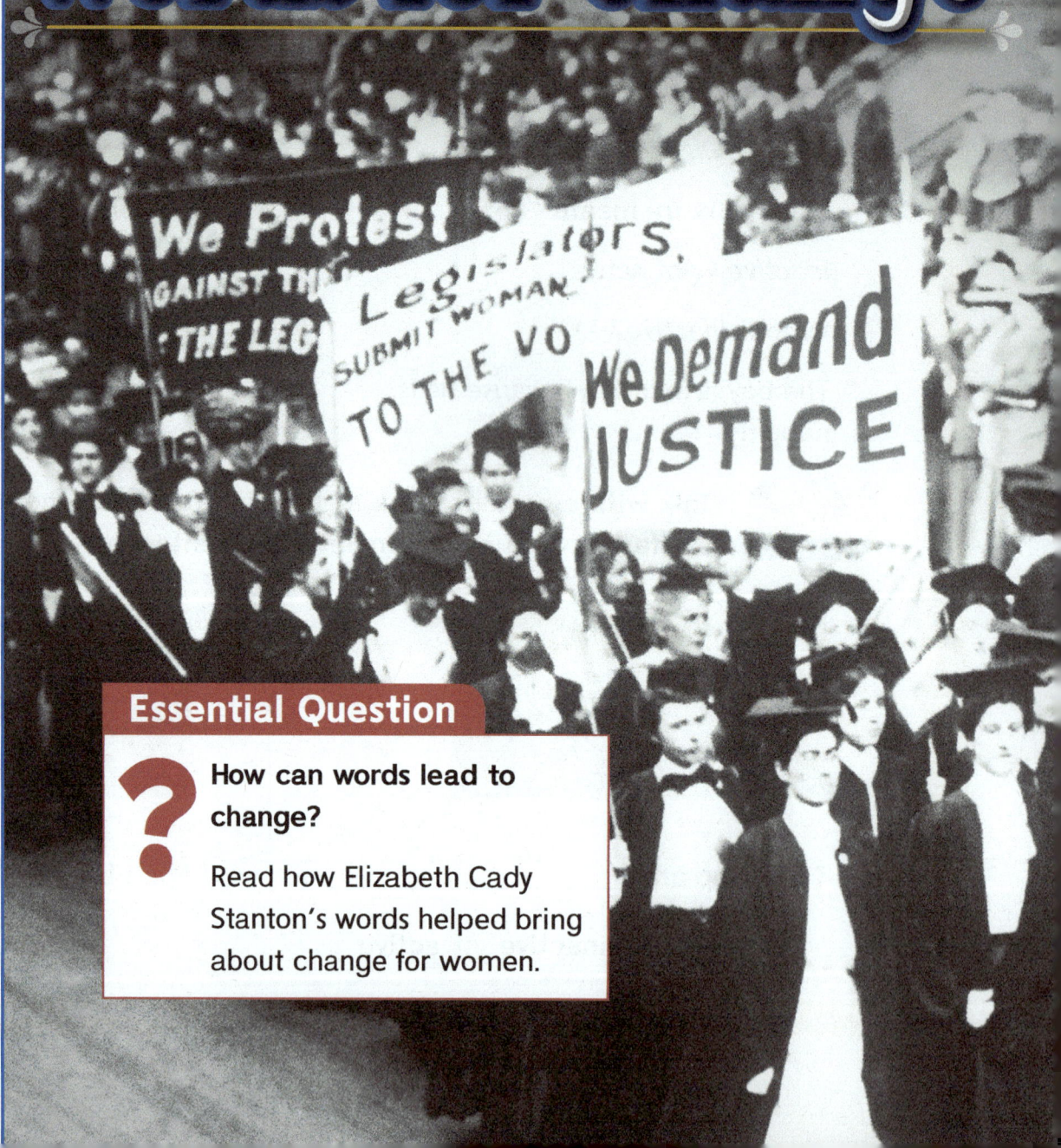

Essential Question

? **How can words lead to change?**

Read how Elizabeth Cady Stanton's words helped bring about change for women.

The Early Years

In 1827, when Elizabeth Cady Stanton was eleven, her father said he wished she were a boy. Elizabeth was hurt. But she was **determined** to prove to her father that women **deserved** the same rights as men.

Elizabeth's father was a lawyer, judge, and congressman. Women came to see him for advice. Her father could not help them because women did not have the same rights as men. Married women could not own property or vote. Elizabeth was upset by the injustice of these laws.

There were many law books in Elizabeth's home. She drew lines through all the laws she did not like. Elizabeth's father told her that she must get lawmakers to pass new laws when she was grown up. Then the unfair laws would disappear. Women's lives would be changed.

Elizabeth Cady Stanton and her daughter

Women march in a parade in New York City.

Text Evidence

1 Specific Vocabulary A C T

Reread the last sentence in the first paragraph. The word *deserved* means "to have earned something." Underline the words that tell what Elizabeth believed women deserved.

2 Sentence Structure A C T

Reread the third sentence in the second paragraph. Circle the word that connects the two parts of the sentence. Underline the part of the sentence that tells why Elizabeth's father could not help the women.

3 Comprehension

Reread the last paragraph. Why did Elizabeth draw lines through law books?

_____

_____

_____.

1 Talk About It

Reread the first paragraph. Discuss how Elizabeth felt about equal rights for African Americans. Elizabeth felt African Americans

should _____

_____.

2 Sentence Structure A C T

Reread the first sentence in the third paragraph. Who does the pronoun *she* refer to?

The pronoun *she* refers to _____.

Underline what she did.

3 Specific Vocabulary A C T

Reread the last paragraph. The word *convention* means a "large meeting where people share the same interests." Circle the words that tell you what this convention was about. Underline the words that tell you what Elizabeth said at the convention.

Working for Change

Elizabeth also felt strongly that African Americans should have equal rights. At the time, the country was divided over the issue of slavery. While working for equal rights, Elizabeth met Henry Stanton. They married in 1840. She **refused** to say "promise to obey" in her wedding vows.

The Seneca Falls Convention

Elizabeth was a wife and a mother. But she also wanted to be an activist and work for change. She wrote a document that stated women should be able to vote and have the same rights as men.

She presented the document in 1848. Elizabeth was at America's first women's rights **convention** in Seneca Falls, New York. Elizabeth and her friend Lucretia Mott organized the event. In Elizabeth's address, she demanded women be given the same rights as men. In her speech, Elizabeth said women should have "all the rights and privileges which belong to them as citizens of the United States."

List of attendees at the convention

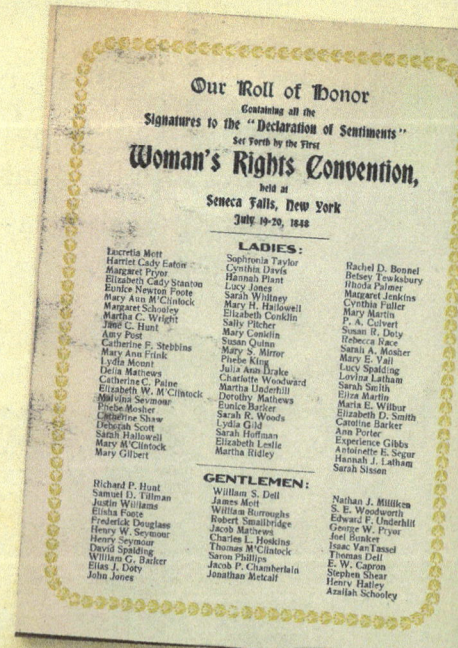

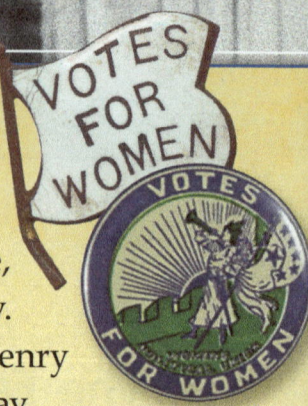

A Winning Team

Elizabeth met Susan B. Anthony in 1851. The two made an **unstoppable** team. They formed the National Woman Suffrage Association in 1869. This group was dedicated to helping women gain the right to vote. Congress was in no hurry to change the law. Elizabeth traveled the country speaking about reforms for women. She did not care if her speeches made some people angry. She believed in her cause.

Susan B. Anthony and Elizabeth Cady Stanton

Victory At Last

Elizabeth Cady Stanton died in 1902. She never got to vote. But her bold words had a lasting effect. Women finally gained the right to vote on August 18, 1920, when the 19th amendment was ratified, or approved. Elizabeth Stanton was a leader for women's rights. And women's lives were changed forever.

Make Connections

? Talk about how Elizabeth Cady Stanton helped women gain the right to vote. **ESSENTIAL QUESTION**

Think about a time when you disagreed with something or wanted to change something. What did you say to try to change it? **TEXT TO SELF**

Text Evidence 🔍

1 **Specific Vocabulary** Ⓐ Ⓒ Ⓣ

Look at the word *unstoppable*. The prefix *un-* means "not" and the suffix *-able* means "able to do something."
What is the meaning of

unstoppable? _____.

2 **Comprehension**
Author's Point of View

Reread the first paragraph. What does the author think about Elizabeth and Susan B. Anthony working together?
The author thinks _____

_____.

COLLABORATE

3 **Talk About It**

Discuss the changes that happened because of Elizabeth's work. Then write about it.

_____

_____

47

Respond to the Text

Partner Discussion Work with a partner. Read the questions about "Words for Change." Show where you found the text evidence. Write the page numbers. Then describe what you learned.

COLLABORATE

What did you learn about Elizabeth when she was young?

I read that Elizabeth's father wished she _____.

Elizabeth was determined to prove to her father that _____.

Elizabeth's father said that when she was grown up she should _____.

Text Evidence 🔍

Page(s): _____

Page(s): _____

Page(s): _____

What did you learn about Elizabeth when she was older?

I read Elizabeth wanted to be an activist to _____.

Elizabeth and Lucretia Mott organized the _____.

Elizabeth wrote a speech and demanded that _____.

Elizabeth's work helped to give women _____.

Text Evidence 🔍

Page(s): _____

Page(s): _____

Page(s): _____

Page(s): _____

Group Discussion Present your answers to the group. Cite text evidence for your ideas. Listen to and discuss the group's opinions about your ideas.

COLLABORATE

I think your idea is _____.

How did Elizabeth Cady Stanton's words bring about change?

Elizabeth Cady Stanton spoke about the need for _____

_____.

She traveled around the country talking about _____

_____.

In 1920, a law was passed that gave _____

_____.

Share Writing Present your writing to the class. Then talk about their opinions. Talk about their ideas. Explain why you agree or disagree with their ideas. You can say:

I agree with _____.

I do not agree because _____.

Write to Sources

pages 44–47

Drew

Take Notes About the Text I took notes on the sequence chart to answer the question: *How did Elizabeth Cady Stanton help women gain equal rights?*

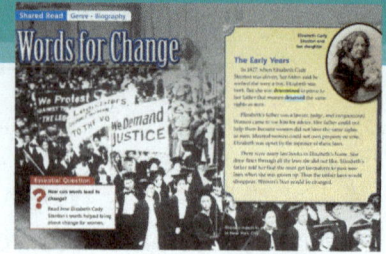

Elizabeth wrote a document. It said that women should have the same rights as men.

⬇

She presented it in 1848.

⬇

She met Susan B. Anthony in 1851. They formed the National Woman Suffrage Association in 1869.

⬇

Elizabeth died in 1902. She never got to vote.

⬇

Women finally gained the right to vote in 1920.

Write About the Text I used the notes from my sequence chart to write about how Elizabeth Cady Stanton helped women gain equal rights.

Student Model: *Informative Text*

Elizabeth Cady Stanton helped women gain equal rights. Elizabeth wrote a document. It said women should have the same rights as men. She presented it in 1848. In 1851, she met Susan B. Anthony. In 1869, they formed the National Woman Suffrage Association. Elizabeth died in 1902. She never got to vote. Women finally gained the right to vote in 1920. Elizabeth had to fight for equal rights for a very long time.

TALK ABOUT IT

COLLABORATE

Text Evidence

Draw a box around a supporting detail from the notes that tells when women gained the right to vote. Does this detail support the conclusion?

Grammar

Circle a past-tense verb. Why did Drew use the past tense to write about Elizabeth?

Condense Ideas

Underline the second and third sentences. How could you combine the sentences into one detailed sentence? You can replace the word *It* with another word.

Your Turn

COLLABORATE

Why did Elizabeth Cady Stanton want equal rights? Use text evidence.

>> *Go Digital*
Write your response online. Use your editing checklist.

Weekly Concept Feeding the World

? **Essential Question**

In what ways can advances in science be helpful or harmful?

>> *Go Digital*

What is the scientist in the photo doing? Describe how science research may help and harm people. Write your ideas in the chart.

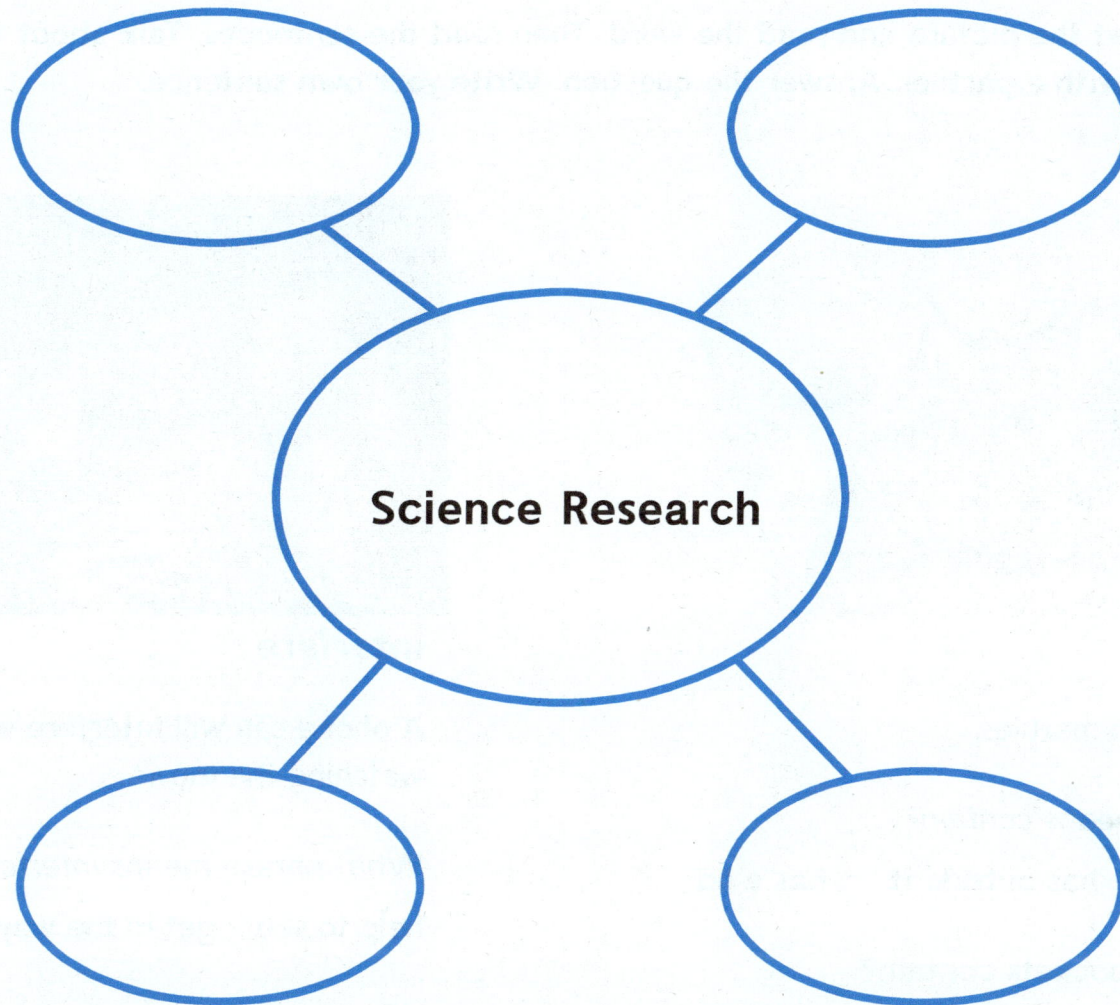

Science Research

Discuss how science can both help and harm people. Use the words from the chart. You can say:

Science can help us because _____.

Science can harm us because _____.

More Vocabulary

Look at the picture and read the word. Then read the sentences. Talk about the word with a partner. Answer the question. Write your own sentence.

contain

The jars **contain** marbles.

What phrase means *contain*?

has inside it   **has outside it**   **has a lid**

What do your pockets contain?

My pockets *contain* _____

_____ .

interfere

A phone call will **interfere** with people watching the movie.

What phrase means *interfere*?

help to see   **get in the way**   **begin to see**

Why does the phone call interfere with the movie?

The phone call will interfere with the movie

because _____

_____ .

Words and Phrases: Multiple-Meaning Word

A multiple-meaning word is a word that can have more than one meaning.

The word *mean* tells about something that is "not nice."

How is the cat acting?

The cat is being **mean** to the dog.

The word *mean* tells what "something describes or tells about."

What is the teacher explaining?

The teacher is explaining what the sentences **mean**.

Talk with a partner. Look at the pictures. Read the sentences. Circle the meaning of the underlined word.

The small dog is <u>mean</u> to the big dog.

not nice   tells about

Clouds usually <u>mean</u> it will rain.

not nice   tells about

(tl)Danielle Donders/Moment Open/Getty Images; (tr)Beathan/SuperStock; (bl)Jodi Jacobson/E+/Getty Images; (br)Jason Weingart Photography

COLLABORATE

① Talk About It

Look at the picture. Read the title. Discuss what you see. Use these words.

scientist   mask   gloves   wheat

Write about what you see.

I see _____

_____.

What is the scientist doing?

The scientist is _____

_____.

What kinds of things can be made from wheat?

The things that can be made from

wheat are _____

_____.

Take notes as you read the text.

Essential Question

? **In what ways can advances in science be helpful or harmful?**

Read about how science has helped to make better food crops.

Food Fight

Is it safe to interfere with Mother Nature?

Something amazing is happening. Some scientists are changing how our food is grown. They are changing the genes of a seed. All living things have genes inside their cells. Genes are arranged into a genetic code. The genetic code controls how a living thing will grow. A seed's genetic code sets the characteristics a plant will have. This could mean that scientists can tell how tall a plant will grow.

For many years, farmers have made crops better by combining them in a process called crossbreeding. They might crossbreed a sweet melon with a big melon. This may produce a big, sweet melon. But the process can take years.

Now, scientists have learned to put a gene from one living thing into another living thing. These foods are called genetically modified foods, or GM foods. GM foods can grow faster and survive insects or bad conditions. But are these changes good for us?

(l) John Lamb/The Image Bank/Getty Images; (tr) Annabelle Breakey/Digital Vision/Getty Images

Text Evidence

1 Specific Vocabulary A C T

Reread the first paragraph. The word *controls* means "has the power to tell how something should be done." Underline the words that tell what a genetic code controls.

2 Sentence Structure A C T

Reread the first sentence in the second paragraph. Underline the punctuation that separates the sentence into two parts. Circle the part of the sentence that tells about time. That part of the sentence is called a prepositional phrase.

COLLABORATE

3 Talk About It

Reread the last paragraph. Discuss what the author says are the good things about GM foods.

GM foods can _____

_____.

Text Evidence 🔍

1 Sentence Structure (A C T)

Reread the third sentence in the first paragraph. What does the pronoun *it* refer to? Find the noun in the second sentence that can replace *it*. Rewrite the sentence using the noun.

_____

_____.

2 Talk About It

Discuss the superfoods in the chart. Describe the kinds of changes scientists have made to the genes of these foods.

3 Specific Vocabulary (A C T)

Reread the last sentence in the last paragraph. The word *nutrient* means "something that will help a plant or animal live and grow." Underline what the nutrient in GM golden rice does that is helpful.

POINT COUNTERPOINT

Support for Superfoods

Scientists have created GM crops that have a resistance to insects and disease. Bt corn is a genetically modified corn. It has a gene that kills insects. Farmers who grow Bt corn can use fewer chemicals. That is good for the farmer and for the environment.

Some GM foods are very good for you. That is why they are called "superfoods." For

Disease-resistant GM potatoes were introduced in the 1990's.

example, golden rice has been genetically modified with three different genes. The new genes make a **nutrient** that prevents some kinds of blindness.

Superfoods

These foods may seem common. But did you know that the genetically modified kinds of these foods have special powers?

Rice

Rice **contains** a kind of acid. Too much acid can be bad for people. A new kind of rice has been made with a low level of the acid.

Salmon

Scientists have changed the gene in salmon that controls growth. The GM salmon grows twice as fast as wild salmon.

Tomatoes

GM tomatoes can be picked when they are ripe and then shipped. And they do not bruise. One company tried to use an arctic fish gene to create a tomato that could survive the cold. But it did not do well.

(t) Peter Dazeley/Photographer's Choice/Getty Images; (br) Stockbyte/Getty Images; (bc) Digital Vision/Getty Images; (bl) Jacques Cornell/McGraw-Hill Education

Hunger in Africa

MAP KEY

Percentage of people that are not getting enough food

- Over 35%
- 20-34%
- 10-19%
- 5-9%
- Less than 5%
- Not enough data

Safety Issues

POINT / COUNTERPOINT

Many people worry GM foods will harm the planet and humans. One **concern** is that GM foods may cause allergies.

Some people will not buy GM foods. As a result, many companies avoid GM foods.

Time Will Tell

Many scientists think any problems with GM foods can be managed. They think it is important to keep researching GM foods because they can help fight the problem of world hunger.

Make Connections

? Talk about the advantages and disadvantages of GM foods. **ESSENTIAL QUESTION**

Would you buy GM foods? **TEXT TO SELF**

1 Specific Vocabulary Ⓐ Ⓒ Ⓣ

Reread the first paragraph. The word *concern* means "something that worries someone." Underline the words that tell what one concern is about GM foods.

2 Comprehension

Author's Point of View

Reread the last paragraph. What does the author think is good about GM foods? Underline the sentence that tells you.

COLLABORATE

3 Talk About It

Discuss the different opinions about GM foods. Then write your opinion about GM foods.

I think GM foods are _____

because _____

_____

_____

_____.

Respond to the Text

COLLABORATE **Partner Discussion** Work with a partner. Read the questions about "Food Fight." Show where you found the text evidence. Write the page numbers. Then describe what you learned.

What are the reasons that GM foods may be helpful?

I read GM foods can _____.

They can also survive _____.

GM golden rice can _____.

Text Evidence

Page(s): _____

Page(s): _____

Page(s): _____

What are the reasons GM foods may be harmful?

I read some people worry that GM foods will _____.

Some people worry GM foods may cause _____.

Many companies avoid GM foods because _____.

Text Evidence

Page(s): _____

Page(s): _____

Page(s): _____

COLLABORATE **Group Discussion** Present your answers to the class. Cite text evidence for your ideas. Listen to and discuss the group's opinions about your ideas.

I think your idea is _____.

Write Work with a partner. Look at your notes about "Food Fight." Then write your answer to the essential question. Use text evidence to support your answer. Use vocabulary words in your writing.

In what ways can GM foods be helpful or harmful?

GM foods can grow _____ and survive

_____.

GM foods may cause harm to the _____ and

_____.

GM golden rice prevents _____.

The author thinks GM foods can help fight the problem of _____.

Share Writing Present your writing to the class. Then talk about their opinions. Talk about their ideas. Explain why you agree or disagree with their ideas. You can say:

I agree with _____.

I do not agree because _____.

Write to Sources

Food Fight

Take Notes About the Text I took notes on the idea web to answer the question: *In your opinion, are GM foods safe?*

pages 56–59

Cristina

Bt corn use fewer chemicals.

Golden rice prevents some blindnesses.

Are GM foods safe?

People worry they may harm the planet and humans.

They may cause allergies.

Write About the Text I used my notes from my idea web to write an opinion about how safe GM foods are to eat.

Student Model: *Opinion*

I think GM foods may not be safe. Too many people worry that GM foods will harm the planet and humans. GM foods may cause allergies. Some GM foods may be helpful like the Bt corn. But I don't think GM foods are safe. People don't know enough about them.

TALK ABOUT IT

Text Evidence

Draw a box around a reason to support Cristina's opinion. Look at the words Cristina used. Does she think GM foods are safe?

Grammar

Circle a word with a suffix. What does the suffix mean?

Connect Ideas

Underline the last two sentences. How can you use the word *because* to connect them?

Your Turn

Does the author think GM foods are a good idea? Use text evidence.

>> Go Digital
Write your response online. Use your editing checklist.